A Year in New York

Elisha Cooper

CITY & COMPANY
NEW YORK

City & Company
22 West 23rd Street
New York, NY 10010

Printed in Hong Kong

Creative Coordinator—Kristin Frederickson
Design by Lia Mariscal

Library of Congress Cataloguing-in-Publication Data
is available upon request.

ISBN 1-885492-24-3

First Edition

for Ovid, my goat

INTRODUCTION

I HAVE AN IDEA: TO WRITE AND PAINT A SKETCHBOOK OF MY
FIRST YEAR IN NEW YORK. FALL, WINTER, SPRING, AND
SUMMER. I'LL GO TO GAMES, SHOWS, CONCERTS, MARKETS, AND
CAFES. TO BROOKLYN, QUEENS, CONEY ISLAND, AND
CHINATOWN. WITH A #5 PENCIL AND MY WATERCOLORS I'LL
WALK AROUND THE STREETS AND POKE INTO AS MANY CORNERS
AS I CAN. I WANT TO SEE WHAT MAKES THIS CITY **SPECIAL**.

Fall

SEPTEMBER 1
TIMES SQUARE

 NINE O'CLOCK ON A MONDAY MORNING.

 IT STARTS  DRIZZLING AS

 COMMUTERS  POUR OUT OF THE SUBWAYS.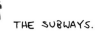

THE MODELS, HIGH ABOVE ON THEIR BILLBOARDS,

SEEM VERY NAKED AND VERY COLD.

SEPTEMBER 3
TAXI CABS

TAXIS LOOK LIKE FROGS TO ME — YELLOW, ROUNDED, BULLFROGS THAT LEAP

I FORGET THAT EACH ONE HAS A HUMAN INSIDE.

12

PAST EACH OTHER DOWN THE STREET. THEY LOOK SO MUCH LIKE ANIMALS

I SIT WITH THE TWO LIONS ON THE PUBLIC LIBRARY STEPS AND WATCH.

A MAN (I THINK) KISSES A WOMAN (I THINK)
AND THEIR WIGS TANGLE.

IN NEW YORK, PEOPLE STAY FOR THE CREDITS.
IT'S A SMALL TIME CONNOISSEURSHIP, WAITING IN THE
EMPTYING BLUE LIGHT OF A THEATER FOR THE
VERY LAST IMAGE, THE LAST DROP OF INFORMATION.
"DID YOU SEE THAT THEY HAD TWO BEE TRAINERS?"

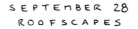

WEST SIDE

BRONX

BROOKLYN

18

OCTOBER 3
WEST 84TH STREET

TWO PORTLY MOVERS SWING BOXES OUT OF THEIR TRUCK. A SPEEDING

TAXIDRIVER CLIPS THEIR SIDE MIRROR; ONE OF THE MEN

LUMBERS AFTER HIM, SHAKING HIS FIST AND BELLOWING.

OCTOBER 9
CARNEGIE HALL

20

FROM OUTSIDE, THE EMPIRE STATE BUILDING IS A NEEDLE ON THE HORIZON. INSIDE, THE CHOIR SINGS "TAKE ME TO THE WATER" AGAIN AND AGAIN WHILE MEN AND WOMEN IN WHITE AND BLACK ROBES ARE DUNKED, BAPTIZED IN A POOL.

ON CENTRAL PARK'S PATHWAYS THIS SUNDAY AFTERNOON, THE WHEELERS AND RUNNERS AND BIKERS ARE A SINGLE CIRCULAR MOVEMENT. IN THEIR RED AND YELLOW SPANDEX SUITS THEY REMIND ME OF A WHIRRING FALL CYCLONE OF LEAVES.

OCTOBER 26
ZABAR'S

ZABAR'S: A MUSEUM TO FOOD. A FRIEND SAYS THE STORE IS MORE
ACCURATELY A GALLERY BECAUSE YOU CAN BUY THE ART. BUT HOW MANY
PEOPLE BUY THINGS AT GALLERIES? I WALK THE AISLES, SMELL, LOOK
AT THE PRICES, AND BUY ONE PUMPKIN TORTELLONI.

23

24

OCTOBER 31
GREENWICH VILLAGE

LIPSTICK

I GO TO NIGHT COURT AT ONE IN THE MORNING — AM STRUCK BY THE BANALITY.
FAMILIES WAIT ON WOODEN BENCHES AS CASES (PEOPLE) FILE IN AND OUT.
A YOUNG BOY DOZES TO MY RIGHT.

NOVEMBER 2
ELECTION DAY

28

NOVEMBER 6
THE MARATHON

A COLD BLUSTERY DAY. POLICEMEN SCRUNCH
THEIR BULL NECKS TIGHT INTO TURNED UP COLLARS.
IF STRINGS WERE ATTACHED TO THEIR FEET,
I WONDER IF THEY'D RISE UP AND FLOAT AWAY.

Winter

I TAKE THE NUMBER SIX TRAIN UP INTO THE BRONX, THEN ALL THE WAY BACK TO MIDTOWN. SNOW SWIRLS OUTSIDE ON THE OPEN PLATFORMS, OCCASIONALLY FINDING ITS WAY THROUGH CRACKS AND ONTO HUDDLED COMMUTERS.

THEY DRIFT IN AND OUT ALSO - FILLING UP THE CAR, MELTING AWAY.

DECEMBER 19
ALVIN AILEY DANCERS

38

ROCKEFELLER CENTER RINK: THE MOST PUBLIC PLACE TO FALL—ESPECIALLY DURING CHRISTMAS, AMIDST THE THRONG OF SHOPPERS AND OGLERS. A WOMAN FLIPS OUT OF HER BALLET TURN ONTO HER BUTT; A MAN DUSTS ICE OFF HIS TAILORED SUIT; A FATHER SUPPORTING HIS TODDLER FALLS HIMSELF.

DECEMBER 23
DOORMEN

ABSOLUTELY POURING. I WALK DOWN FIFTH AVENUE FROM THE METROPOLITAN AND BY 75TH ST. I'M SOAKED. FROM ACROSS THE STREET I SEE THAT THE DOORMEN ARE DRY. THEY CROUCH UNDER AWNINGS AND VENTURE OUT ONLY UNDER OVERSIZE UMBRELLAS.

1035

955

923

900

860

DECEMBER 24
SAKS FIFTH AVENUE

THE LINE FOR THE WOMEN'S BATHROOM AT THE MET IS OVER SIXTY FEET LONG.
I PACE IT OUT CAREFULLY. HEEL, TOE, HEEL, TOE. MEASURING MY
FEET, COUNTING MY STRIDES — SIXTY FEET. THAT'S A LONG LINE.

JANUARY 5
CENTRAL PARK ZOO

THE ZOO IS JUMPING.
WHILE THE TEMPERATURE
DROPS, POLAR BEARS PLAY

(TWO PLASTIC
BLOCKS AND AN
ORANGE BALL).

THEY SEEM TO BE
THE ONLY ONES HAPPY
WITH THE LOUSY WEATHER.

45

JANUARY 10
GRAND CENTRAL

I'M IN GRAND CENTRAL,
LATE. A YOUNG MAN RUNS
INTO THE ROTUNDA,
GLANCES QUICKLY AT

THE FLICKERING BOARD. THEN
BOUNDS — SLAP SLAP SLAP —
ACROSS THE MARBLE FLOOR

TO TRACK 17, ONLY TO
GLIMPSE THE TAIL OF THE
1:20 RETREAT UP ITS TUNNEL.

HANDS ON HEAD, HE STOPS, THEN
SLUMPS SLOWLY TO THE STAIRS
WHERE HE SITS, AND WAITS.

46

47

JANUARY 19
LATE SHOW WITH DAVID LETTERMAN

"WHEN IT LIGHTS UP, YOU CLAP!" SAYS THE WRITER WARMING UP THE CROWD WHILE POINTING AT THE "APPLAUSE" SIGN.

DURING BREAKS IN THE SHOW, DAVE PUFFS ON A CIGAR, FEET UP, AND YAKS WITH A PRODUCER.

I CAN'T SEE A THING.

WHEN THE NEXT GUEST COMES ON, CAMERAS CONVERGE ON LETTERMAN AND BLOCK HIM FROM THE AUDIENCE.

THE DRUMMERS RACK THEIR STICKS AGAINST THE CORRUGATED METAL DOOR BEHIND THEM.

DUM, DA DA DUM BADA DUM, RRRRRRIP, RRRRRRIP.

FEBRUARY 8
MADISON SQUARE GARDEN

THE TICKET I SCALP IS COUNTERFEIT
BOUGHT IT FROM ASSURED ME
TALKING MY WAY IN. NOTHING DOING.
FOR GOOD, I ASK HER? FIVE MINUTES
KNICKS, SITTING NEXT TO HER

(THOUGH THE NICE MAN I
OTHERWISE). I TRY SWEET-
THEN I SEE A WOMAN LEAVING.
LATER, I'M WATCHING THE
FATHER-IN-LAW.

EIGHT O'CLOCK ON A
SPORTS DESK PUMPED!
ON MSG. THE BIG RANGERS
AND GREASY DISHES OF
WHAT COULD

SUNDAY NIGHT, AND BOY IS THE
THEY GOT THE KNICKS RUNNING
GAME COMING UP AT SEVEN,
GREEK SALAD BEHIND THEM.
BE BETTER?

FEBRUARY 22
CANAL STREET

52

MARCH 10
MESSENGERS

MARCH 25
FASHION SHOOT

AT FIRST THEY SEEM LIKE
PEOPLE. BUT AFTER TAKING
OFF T-SHIRTS, FLIPPING
AWAY SNEAKERS, JUMPING

HAIR

INTO PURPLE SUITS AND
COMBING THEIR HAIR
WET, THEY BECOME
MODELS — AND TAKE
OVER BOTH PATHS ON
THE BROOKLYN BRIDGE.

SOCKS

PASSING BICYCLISTS
BLOW WHISTLES AND
SHAKE FISTS.

58

FOR A WHOLE WEEK I WORK EVERY ANGLE TO GET INTO
THE SEVENTH ON SIXTH FASHION SHOW IN BRYANT
PARK. NO LUCK. SO I DRAW PEOPLES' SHOES INSTEAD.

APRIL 9
HUDSON RIVER

TUGBOATS, FROM WHERE I STAND IN HOBOKEN, LOOK LIKE COLORFUL SCOOTING BUGS.

COLORFUL, NOT VERY ENERGETIC TUGS, MOVING SLOWLY ACROSS THE WATER.

I NOTICE WRISTS; BENT, TURNING, ELONGATED. HANDS CRADLING COFFEE, TOUCHING A STRAW, HOLDING A CIGARETTE. THE GESTURES OF THESE CAFE PEOPLE ARE LIKE SOME SEDENTARY DANCE.

APRIL 20
ST. MARKS-IN-THE-BOWERIE

ALLEN GINSBERG ALMOST
STEPS ON MY FOOT

AS I STAND BY THE DOOR OF THE
JOHN ASHBERY POETRY READING.

IN THE MIDDLE OF
ONE READING

A CAT RUSHES
THE PODIUM.

ALLEN
GINSBERG

GINSBERG,
AGAIN

APRIL 29
BELMONT PARK

ON THE TARMAC OF THE INFIELD OF BELMONT PARK
I FIND CRUSHED CANS, BOTTLE CAPS, CRUSHED
PEANUTS, NACHOS, RIPPED "AUTOTOTE" RACING
TICKETS, SHREDDED RACING FORMS, SMUSHED CIGAR
ENTRAILS (LOTS OF THESE), URINE, AND EVEN
A PUDDLE OF BLOOD, STILL WET.

MAY 3
RANGERS STANLEY CUP CELEBRATION

LETS GO
RANGERS

I GO TO A FISHMARKET ON THE CORNER OF LAFAYETTE AND CANAL. FIVE MEN WITH APRONS AND TAN RUBBER GLOVES CRAM FISH ONTO CRATES OF ICE. THEY WORK ROUGHLY, QUICKLY, WITH NO EXCESS MOTION. ONE FISH SLIPS TO THE PAVEMENT, IS PICKED UP, PUT BACK. ONE SELLER SMOKES, ANOTHER FARMER BLOWS HIS NOSE ON THE FLOOR.

MAY 19
UNION SQUARE GREENMARKET

I BUY A BUNCH OF BASIL AND HOLD IT LIKE A BOUQUET WITH MY NOSE STUFFED
INSIDE. AS I WAIT ON THE SUBWAY PLATFORM FOR MY TRAIN (NOSE IN BASIL),
THREE DIFFERENT PEOPLE APPROACH AND ASK ME WHAT IT IS.

MAY 27
SHEEP MEADOW

WALKING UP THE EAST SIDE THIS SPRING NIGHT, I SEE A COUPLE MAKING OUT - <u>REALLY</u> GOING AT IT. I STOP TO TIME THEM AS MY FRIENDS MOVE ON.

FORTY-FIVE SECONDS LATER THE COUPLE'S STILL KISSING. WOW!

IN SOHO, I CAN'T TELL THE DIFFERENCE

BETWEEN THE ART GALLERIES AND

THE SHOE STORES. THEY BOTH HAVE SUCH

BEAUTIFULLY POLISHED WOOD FLOORS.

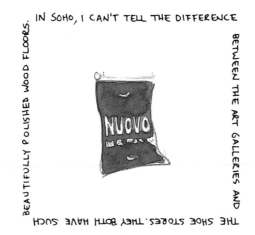

Summer

JUNE 16
BRYANT PARK

79

WOOFING, WEAVING, WOOFING, SLAPPING, WOOFING, SLAMMING.
OCCASIONALLY PULLING SHORTS UP TO THE BOTTOMS OF THEIR ASSES.
HOW IS IT THEY DON'T TRIP?

JUNE 27
CENTRAL PARK

THE NEW YORKER PLAYS THE WALL STREET JOURNAL. MOST PEOPLE STAND AROUND AND DRINK.

JULY 2
CONEY ISLAND

I PUSH MY WAY PAST BEER CANS, PLASTIC BAGS, AND DIAPERS, AND WADE OUT INTO THE WATER. BOBBING THROUGH

SMALL WAVES, I FEEL LIKE A SEAL. WHEN I POKE MY NOSE UP THROUGH

THE WATER I CAN SEE THE ROLLER COASTERS.

JULY 4
JONES BEACH

JULY 13

SAHADI IMPORTING, BROOKLYN

BACLAVA

A SWELTERING DAY.

I WANDER THE

STREETS OF

BROOKLYN TRYING

TO STAY ON THE

SHADY SIDE OF

THE STREET.

A HYDRANT

IS OPENED

AND A COMMUNITY

CARWASH

IS BORN.

AUGUST 6
WASHINGTON SQUARE PARK

SLAP!

CHECK!

AUGUST 15
LAFAYETTE STREET

EARLY MORNING IN
THE EAST
VILLAGE. SUN
COMING UP.

GASORAMA

149

MECHANICS'
HANDS MESH
WITH PARTS.
WHEN THEY

THEY ARE BODIES
JOINED — MEN WITH
CARHEADS.

RETREAT UNDER THE
BELLIES OF CARS

89

AUGUST 18
YANKEE STADIUM

Getty

yellow

blue

90

I LISTEN TO SOUNDS AT
YANKEE STADIUM. THE DIALOGUE
OF REAL FANS - "MATTINGLY, YOU
SUUUUUCK," THE CALL OF VENDORS, "COLD
BEYAH, HEYAH," THE OCCASIONAL RUMBLE OF THE #4
TRAIN PAST THE OUTFIELD, THE ORGAN, THE CRACK AS A
FOUL BALL CAREENS INTO THE GRANDSTAND....

AUGUST 27
FRISBEE

EVERY SUNDAY AT ONE O'CLOCK I PLAY ULTIMATE

GIRLS LEAPING AFTER A

MUDDY AND FEELING HAPPY, I PAUSE

FRISBEE IN THE PARK AT 97TH. GOOFY GUYS AND DISK AND KICKING UP DIRT. GRASS STAINED, BRUISED, AND SKETCH MY FRIENDS.

AUGUST 29
WEST 44TH STREET

AND NOW IT'S BEEN A YEAR. A FALL OF MARATHONS, A WINTER OF

SLUSH, A SPRING FULL OF FRISBEES, AND A SUMMER PERPETUALLY

IN SEARCH OF COOL AND WATER: THE RHYTHMS OF A CITY.

SOMETIMES I KNOW WHERE I'M GOING, OTHER TIMES THINGS COME

TO ME AND I'M LEFT FUMBLING FOR MY PENCIL (QUICK!).

NEW YORK IS WHAT'S AROUND THE NEXT CORNER.

ABOUT THE AUTHOR

Elisha Cooper grew up in Connecticut,
played football at Yale, then worked as
a messenger for The New Yorker magazine.
He is twenty-four years old.